NO LAMB SO BEAUTEOUS
AND OTHER CHRISTMAS POEMS

KEVIN CAREY

ILLUSTRATED BY KEVIN SHEEHAN

Sacristy
Press

Sacristy Press
PO Box 612, Durham, DH1 9HT

www.sacristy.co.uk

First published in 2013 by Sacristy Press, Durham

Copyright © Kevin Carey 2013
The right of Kevin Carey to be identified as the author of
this work has been asserted by him in accordance with
the Copyright, Designs and Patents Act 1988.

Illustrations Copyright © Kevin Sheehan 2013

All rights reserved, no part of this publication may be reproduced
or transmitted in any form or by any means, electronic,
mechanical photocopying, documentary, film or in any other
format without prior written permission of the publisher.

Sacristy Limited, registered in England & Wales, number 7565667

British Library Cataloguing-in-Publication Data
A catalogue record for the book is available from the British Library

ISBN 978-1-908381-21-7

www.jesus4u.co.uk

CONTENTS

Preface v
Musical Settings vi

No Lamb So Beauteous 1
The Apple... 7
Bible Dance 8
Salvation's Dam... 9
Mary Was Dreaming 10
The Baptist Cries.. 11
O Come Emmanuel, Come! 11
Stroll-Along Donkey 12
For Our Little Lamb...................................... 13
The Lover.. 14
How Dark the Sky 14
No Halo 15
Silent Night 16
When Jesus Came.. 18
Sleep, Little Darling 19
Sing Noel 20
Come and See! 21
A Child of Blood and Fire................................ 22
Fleeter than Donkeys 23
The Christmas Show 24
Difference 25
Askew.. 26
A Strange Story.. 27
On Christmas Night....................................... 28
Sheep 29

iii

Snow	30
Desert Ships	32
Children	33
Nature	34
Prophesies	35
Going Back	36
Post-Epiphany Carols	38
Honour All	41
Bring Your Candles	42
Simeon's Death	43
Solidarity	44
The Apple Wood of Calvary	45
Pageant	46
If I Could Wish	47
Then and Now	48
They Brought Jesus!	49
Good Cheer!	50
The Rose	52
Mistletoe and Holly	53
Petals	54
Virgin of the Raj	55
On Beauty	56
Christmas Town	58
Mary's Child	59

PREFACE

Whether or not it is a late flowering or a harbinger of new growth, the abundance of contemporary church music on both sides of the Atlantic is as startling as was its late nineteenth-century English revival. With the rise of popular church music in the late 1960s it appeared as if the tradition from Stainer to Britten might be at an end, but we are now enjoying a period of substantial and eclectic output from jazz to the crypto-medieval. Nowhere is this variety more evident than in the range of new Christmas music from, to name some leading carol composers, John Rutter, Andrew Carter, Morton Lauridsen, Malcolm Archer, Bob Chilcott, and Eric Whitacre.

Yet, no matter how skilled the musician, there comes a point at which new lyrics are required. Many of the most popular carols already have such traditionally favoured settings that any new attempt frequently sounds like novelty for its own sake; and as the years go by an ever greater number of lyrics receive what become classic settings where novelty is hard to imagine. For example, there is the case of Harold Darke's setting of Christina Rossetti's *In the Bleak Midwinter* which far surpasses the earlier and, in its day very popular, Holst setting and although there are hundreds of settings of *O Magnum Mysterium* it is hard to see Morton Lauridsen's recent setting becoming outmoded.

If the carol setting tradition is to survive, new lyrics are wanted as the old become ever more associated with one or two settings. I first became aware of this need when learning Howells' *Here is the Little Door* and ever since it has been my hope to offer contemporary composers new possibilities.

In this second collection of Christmas poetry I have quite deliberately followed the broad pattern of the first, laying out my pieces in approximate chronological order, starting and concluding with a set of pieces suitable for an extended work for choir and soloists. Readers might also notice a bias towards the archaic which, I believe, matches the zeitgeist for an approach nearer to the Medieval than the Victorian.

Meanwhile, although I hope that composers will contact the publisher if they wish to set any of these pieces, I am conscious that the much greater audience will be the general reader seeking a different perspective on what has for many become a somewhat hackneyed festival which is a pity when the birth of any child, but this child in particular, is so special.

Kevin Carey
Hurstpierpoint, West Sussex
Trinity Sunday 2013

MUSICAL SETTINGS

These lyrics were written both for reading and for setting to music. The first poem, *No Lamb So Beauteous*, is in several parts. It is intended that they are set as follows: (i) choir; (ii) sopranos/altos; (iii) soprano or alto; (iv) men; (v) choir; (vi) baritone; (vii) choir. *When Jesus Came* (p. 18) is to be set in 3/4 time.

My translation of Mohr's *Silent Night* (p. 16) is not completely literal, but is much closer than the popular Freeman Young version which uses verses 1, 6 and 2 of Mohr; the translation is also limited by my assumption that almost everyone will want a version to fit Gruber's melody.

The author would be very pleased to hear from composers who may be interested in setting any of these lyrics. Please contact the publisher if you would like to do so.

NO LAMB SO BEAUTEOUS

i.

The whole world groans in anguish for the day
When our Creator's promise will be kept
That we, unbound from Adam's bondage may
Become, once tarnished vessels, cleaned and swept.
The days grow darker outside and within,
Oppression's burden crowned with anxious hope,
Our cheerfulness grows brittle, sharp and thin,
The best that we can manage is to cope.

Yet that which is most brittle shines most bright,
Its glittering teases as the day draws near;
Redemption, once miasma, comes in sight,
Impatience knuckles loose the bonds of fear:
Lord Jesus come, come quickly down to earth,
Dispel our gloom with infant cries of peace,
Reward our fickle patience with your birth,
Fulfil the long-held promise of release.

ii.

Against the darkening Winter wind
A donkey slithers down the stones
Sharpening her pain,
Sapping youth's vibrancy,
Reducing her to aching flesh and bones.

Lamps lure the beast and stay the pain,
The spitting welcome brings relief;
Callous disdain,
Equivocating pregnancy,
The outcast straw, strewn roughly, softens grief.

Low cries the child, too weak for lust,
Too slight to bear the sloth and crime,
Born to sustain
Incarnate mystery:
The shadow of the Cross falls back in time.

iii.

So far away the angel's message sounds
As restless soldiers tramp the market place;
I wonder if I dreamed that miracle
Or harbour a delusion of my grace.

Perhaps it is the fire in my womb
Extinguished by cold terror in my breast
Which assuages and torments me by turns:
But for the moment, Lord, just give us rest.

Enough of introspection's ebb and flow,
However formed and born, he is my son,
I am the only mother that he knows,
And we will finish what we have begun.

iv.

Not like the shepherds we have heard of Greece,
From travellers' tales,
Lush grass and blooming maidens
Gaudy of attire and gifted
In the Terpsichorean art:

Ours is a parched life, sparse
And outcast of the supple softness of caress:
Bound to our spindly sheep and yet
We love them as if their fleeces
Were fit for palaces.

But Grecians never heard such thunderous choirs,
Of angels far surpassing their mean lyres;
No messenger of Zeus has ever brought,
Such joyful news to meeting house and court:
No lamb so beauteous, worthy to adorn
The crib of this sweet child, Messiah born.

V.

Mysterious tidings billow round the inn,
Shepherds are feted then despised;
The subjects of their gossip darkly fled,
The angel vaulted hope unrealised.
What of mysterious omens in the sky?
Hope always vanquished by despair,
The bane of drudgery ruts palsied breasts
Dissolving promises in fetid air.

Insinuating rumours breed mistrust;
What is the crime? Who is to blame?
The questions are redundant as the guilty
And the innocent will be treated just the same.

vi.

His eyes light with the glitter of strange gold
As agents tally cargo at the gate;
But darken as his courtiers relate
What prophets and these men have both foretold:
Yet cunning glues him to his fragile throne;
His undeceiving smile sends them away
Knowing the court he promises to pay
Will be to himself or will not be done.
They drop their gifts in haste and fluff their lines
And, well advised, shun Herod's courtesy;
The slaughter was not foretold in the signs,
Nor why the child was worth such cruelty:
But wisdom's pride and arms which make a king
Will be transformed by this child's suffering.

vii.

'A Life' confined to childhood yields small truths;
The manger teaches but the Cross restores;
God in our flesh breaks into time and space
But victory over death destroys all laws.

For we will die in Christ awaiting him
To end this world and heaven, to re-create
Our selves complete in corporate harmony
With God and humankind in perfect state.

THE APPLE

Adam lived in a garden
And it was fair and green;
And God gave him a maiden,
The fairest ever seen:
And all that marred their pleasure
Was a shining apple gold
That they were not to eat of
As our Creator told.

But as soon as they had eaten
The sweet to bitter turned;
And God stern said to Adam
Your victuals must be earned
And as for you, so tempted,
New life will bring you pain
And between you and the serpent
An issue will remain.

But slithered up the serpent
And said to comely Eve,
This fruit will never harm you
But bless you, I believe:
For you will have the knowledge
As adults to behave;
And remain as children
As God says he would have.

But then was born a maiden
Spotless and fair as Eve,
Visited by an angel
Who said she would conceive:
And give to us a saviour
True God and yet true man:
To free us of the apple
Where our sorrows began.

BIBLE DANCE

Adam for an apple paid with every human life
Eve for eating paid in pain for every bearing wife:
Abraham who gave his son was chosen of the Lord:
Moses led his people out across the Red Sea ford.

Isaiah promised after pain the people would be free
Through a king he said would spring from the root of Jesse,
Cousin John at the Jordan said make the crooked straight
Here he comes, the Lamb of God, for whom all people wait.

He was born in Bethlehem where Jesse had his flocks
Shepherds came who heard his fame, warmed by the ass and ox
Angels bright that starry night proclaimed goodwill to men
But infants were the first to die for what wise men had seen.

Maiden servant killed a serpent down in Bethlehem
Apple tree to Calvary the wood was yet the same
God, Adam and Abraham at last all shared a son
And Jesus Christ the source of life ended what they began.

SALVATION'S DAM

The Baptist cries against the wind,
His rough words blown back in his face,
He sees the inward, sinful mind,
They see his obvious disgrace.

And were he to walk down our street
Shouting aloud our faithless sin,
The priest and wardens would retreat,
Determined not to let him in.

But he it was who saw the Lamb,
Making himself the first but least,
Breaching the sacramental dam
To watch salvation being released.

MARY WAS DREAMING

Mary was dreaming of her love,
Fitfully working at her loom,
Blinked as the sun which glared so bright
Flooded her dark and tiny room.

When she looked up, an angel stood
Towering above her frightened head,
"Mary, all hail, the blessed one,
I come from God," the angel said.

"You have been chosen of your race,
Infused with grace to bear a son,
He comes to save the poor and weak
He is the Lord, the holy one."

"God's will is mine," the young girl said,
"I am his handmaid, mine his womb."
"Farewell," the angel, parting, said,
Leaving her in the darkened room.

THE BAPTIST CRIES

The Baptist cries, the Virgin prays,
Life quickens with Isaiah;
Eyes bright, we count the shortest days
Waiting for the Messiah:

The purple of our penitence
Confronts our sinfulness
Threatened by scarlet opulence
Plunging into excess:

Darkness alive with candle flame
Lit by the Spirit's fire;
Our Saviour born in seeming shame
Child of sublime desire.

O COME EMMANUEL, COME!

O come, Emmanuel, come!
Our vigil is too long,
What we began with flame
Is now a sad song:

That clear but distant ray
Is fogged with earthly greed,
And with each desperate day
You are our need.

The stately Advent road
Is cluttered with the mess
Of human appetites.
Be our excess.

Their baby is the end;
Christ's wreath will be a crown
Of thorns then heavenly bliss;
Emmanuel, come down!

STROLL-ALONG DONKEY

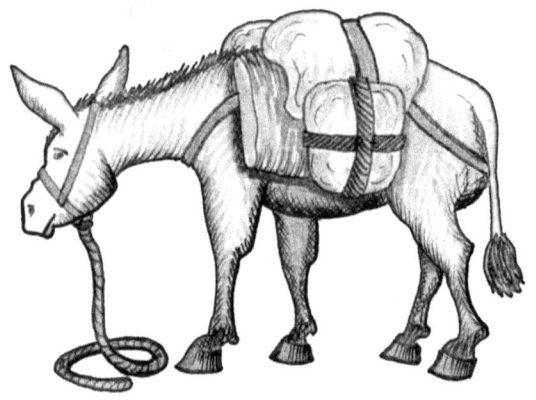

Stroll-along donkey
Who are you carrying today,
Stroll-along donkey,
As you plod your weary way?
The lady with her load
Is slight to carry
But stroll-along,
Do not hurry!

Stroll-along donkey
I know the hay is thin and worn,
Stroll-along donkey,
At least the stall is clean and warm:
The baby in the straw
Is extraordinary,
But stroll-along
Do not worry.

Stroll-along donkey,
So Egypt took you by surprise,
Stroll-along donkey,
Look at the fear in their eyes:
The baby on your back
Is extraordinary,
So stroll-along donkey
Hurry! Hurry!

FOR OUR LITTLE LAMB

Light a candle
For the window
As a signal
Of our yearning,
For our little lamb
Before the year's turning.

Cut the gifts for
Those with plenty,
Fill the stockings
Of the empty
For our little lamb
So poor and so lowly.

Say a quiet prayer
For the gentle
But eschew the
Sentimental
For our little lamb
So meek was slaughtered.

THE LOVER

I sat on a rock with the wind blowing wild
And saw a young girl full ripe with a child
Pass by on a donkey with the night closing in,
Her husband so old that I thought it a sin.

I carried a flagon for the company's cheer
And heard a loud groaning which filled me with fear;
I peeped through the slats, and a baby I spied,
That young girl looked down and the baby he cried.

I walked through the night time to rid me of woe
For my sweetheart had sworn that she loved me not so;
And angels sang comfort for such as me poor
And I thought of my maiden; and our love evermore.

HOW DARK THE SKY

How dark the sky,
How bright the star:
The soldier's tread,
The tavern's roar,
Destined to praise
A child so poor,
Lord Jesus born
for us all.

How dark the sky
Shot through with light:
The shepherd's dull
And angels bright
Worship the child
On this great night,
Lord Jesus born
for us all.

How dark the sky,
The comet's tail
Draws camels onward
Like a sail
At God's command,
They cannot fail
Lord Jesus born
for us all.

NO HALO

No halo but his freezing breath,
The star shine was the only light;
In birth so very near to death,
An outcast on that Winter night.

The grizzled shepherds, bent and thin,
Not lusty youths of rustic charm,
Their pipes a melancholy din,
Breaking what sense there was of calm.

The kings brought torment with their gifts,
Herod's scent clinging to their hair,
His words encoded in their shifts
From reverence to abject fear.

But is our welcome, bright and shrill,
What he would want, who lay so low?
And are our tidings of goodwill,
A parody of long ago?

SILENT NIGHT

1. Silent night! Holy night!
See their lone vigil bright:
See the holy and intimate pair,
Lovely child with curly hair;
Sleep in heavenly peace!

2. Silent night! Holy night!
Son of God, pure delight:
Love and Laughter illumine his face,
Stunning us with his saving grace
From the hour of his birth.

3. Silent night! Holy Night!
Graces our earthly plight:
From heaven's golden heights his birth
Pours God's mercy on the earth:
God in Jesus seen!

4. Silent night! Holy night!
Father's love, power and might
Given today to the human race
In the arms of a child's embrace:
Jesus for the whole world

5. Silent night! Holy Night!
Ancient plans put things right:
We are freed from the exile of wrong
Foretold throughout the ages long:
Saviour of the whole world.

6. Silent night! Holy night!
Shepherds first saw the light;
Sounding forth both near and far
Heard the angels' alleluia
Our Saviour Jesus is here!

WHEN JESUS CAME

Over the hills came the wind with a sweep,
Ruffling the hair of the boy in his sleep,
Counting a fortune of heavenly sheep
When Jesus came.

Standing before him an angel in white
Woke him from sleep with a terrible fright:
Unearthly voice and clothes unearthly bright:
When Jesus came.

"Don't be afraid, I bring news of a birth,"
Good news for all of goodwill upon earth
But, most of all, pilgrims who suffered a dearth
Before He came.

Smiling, she beckoned them to take a peep
At their saviour lying before them asleep,
King of creation, including the sheep
When Jesus came.

SLEEP, LITTLE DARLING

Sleep, little darling, till the dawn,
Now that the shepherds' song is done;
Snuggle the lamb to keep you warm,
Joseph will keep you safe from harm.

Sleep in the straw, so sweet but rough,
It is the best that we can do;
Life will be turbulent enough,
If what the angels say is true.

Yours is the glory, ours the pain,
Worthy when you become a man,
Until you seek my breast again,
Sleep, little darling, while you can.

SING NOEL

Sing Noel
Ring the bell
News to tell
All is well.

Angel shows	Shepherds keep	Wise men see
Spirit knows	Flocks of sheep	Christ to be
Baby grows	Take a peep	Reverently
Heals our woes.	Babe asleep.	Bend the knee.
Sing Noel . . .	*Sing Noel . . .*	*Sing Noel . . .*

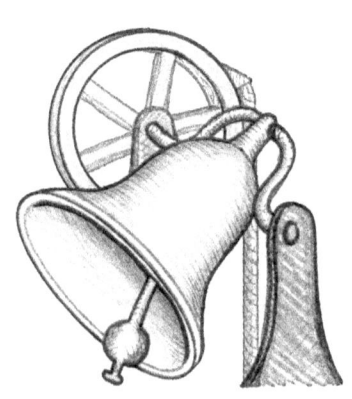

COME AND SEE!

Once on a day
Our Saviour Christ was born:
Come and see! Come and see!
Born in a stable
Cold and all forlorn:
Jesus is born
For all today:
Come and pray! Come and pray.

Once on a night
The shepherds heard the word:
Come and see! Come and see!
He is the good news,
He is Christ the Lord:
Come and see! Come and see!
Jesus is born
For all today
Come and pray!
Come and pray.

Always forever
Christ was born for us:
Thank the Lord! Thank the Lord!
Hung on the cross
And yet victorious:
Thank the Lord! Thank the Lord!
Risen, triumphant,
From the straw!
Alleluia!

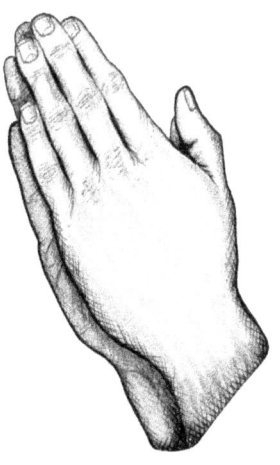

A CHILD OF BLOOD AND FIRE

Along the rough and winding road
A laden donkey bears its load
Of mother and Messiah;
A child of blood and fire.

Within a dark and musty shed
A manger never meant as bed
Bears God incarnate
In his helpless state.

Yet scrawny sheep in scrawny fields
With scanty fare and scanty yields
Are fat with jubilation:
And loud with celebration.

Beneath a brightly shining star
The weary scholars from afar
Are bent on admiration:
But bend in adoration.

FLEETER THAN DONKEYS

Fleeter than donkeys plod,
Faster than shepherds, I
Am the first to see God,
Out of the angel sky.

Sometimes the glow in coal,
Sometimes the cooing dove;
Wrongly described as soul
When I am active love.

Shimmer the sudden star,
Signal the angel song,
Gone from the seminar
Into the mess of things gone wrong.

Father and me in Christ;
Flesh in the Trinity,
Unable to resist
The love of humanity.

THE CHRISTMAS SHOW

There is no snow to cloak the barren rocks,
Blurring the outlines of the scrawny flocks;
The wind shifts from a whisper to a shout,
The rain seems not to pacify the drought.

He shall not want that picturesque display
Of passing beauty, soon grown thin and grey;
But songs of sheltering shepherds at the gate,
Grumbling at wind and weather as they wait.

For nature's core is not the high romance
Of peak and glade, but human circumstance;
The beauty of his birth lies in its mess,
The ingrained human trait of incompleteness.

Of craft and artifice, there was the trough,
Where he was laid in coarse but wholesome cloth,
The star that hovered over Bethlehem,
The nearest form of brightness to a gem.

But can we bear the lash of wind and rain,
His cold so close to death where he was lain?
Or shall we keep the sheen of perfect snow,
The sentimental, pretty Christmas show?

DIFFERENCE

Like the sun when fog has cleared
Like young love that knows no blight
You are new wine, the cup that cheers
   You are the candle in the night.

Like an unflawed amethyst
Like a lake both deep and clear
You born lowly are the Christ
Who feels our pain and knows our fear.

Like the Mona Lisa's smile
Like Beethoven's uncorked zest
Change more disruptive than style
Rapture that could not be guessed.

You are freedom newly known
You are news uniquely good
The only perfect thing we own
Our God made known in flesh and blood.

ASKEW

Ragged myrtle hedge,
Icicles askew,
Snow blurring the edge,
Snow blurring the view:

On Christmas night
Of star-shine bright:
Church bells ringing,
Angels singing.

Shepherds warbling pipe,   Grumpy camels pad
Frightened, scattered sheep,   Through the baking sand,
Shuffling in the street,   Careworn kings press on
Nobody can sleep: Through the hostile land:

On Christmas night . . .   *On Christmas night . . .*

Red and purple meet
Lit by pagan light,
A baby's birth brings joy
On a Winter's night:

On Christmas night . . .

A STRANGE STORY

Whoever heard of a king in a stable?
Unless, of course, he was patting his horse;
And whoever brackets shepherds with angels?
Well, perhaps you may if you're writing a play.
And when have kings knelt at the bed of an infant
Unless they are settling dynastic affairs?
All these improbable things in one story
Told down the ages for two thousand years.

A king in a manger surrounded by shepherds
Is as wild as a king nailed to die on a cross;
And a king in a hut sought by exotic strangers
Is as strange as a gift from a corporate boss;
But of all of the strange things told in Jesus' story
The strangest of all is God's life on our earth
To express solidarity with our dilemmas
In spite of the fact that we put him to death.

ON CHRISTMAS NIGHT

A baby is sleeping in the tinsel,
A candle glows weakly in the light,
The sleigh bells are drowning out the angels,
On Christmas night.

An orphan forgets his life of squalor,
A ragged girl looks for something bright,
A foreman gives out an extra dollar
On Christmas night.

A prisoner feels starlight in the darkness,
An exile is home and all feels right,
The world for a moment is united
On Christmas night.

SHEEP

The notes of a thin pipe falter
As the dull evening meets its end;
Brush for a make-shift shelter
Not a match for the cruel wind:
The spindly sheep stand huddled,
Grown tired of the withered grass;
The men and their flock all anxious
For the threat of the night to pass.

The voice of an angel pierced their sleep
And they woke in a blazing light;
"Good news," said the angel, "Goodwill to all men,"
But his comfort filled them with fright:
Then they heard a choir singing
With a sweetness unknown before,
And they saw the lambs all dancing,
And they praised God for what they saw.

The baby laid in the manger
Hardly looked like an infant king;
But their simple faith did not waver
As they made him their offering:
Their puzzled leader marvelled
That the fleece was so rich and deep;
The good news had clearly favoured
The poor shepherds and their sheep.

SNOW

Cruel as the snow is beautiful
    The virgin carpet spreads before the virgin bride,
Cold as the wind is clinical
    It grimly ransacks treasured warmth from every side:

Yet deep within her heart she feels the pain
Of labour, love and loss she can't explain.

Harsh as the inn is welcoming,
    The outcasts pay above the tariff to get in;
Bare as the cave is comforting,
    She knows her first great love is destined to begin:

Yet in the darkness of the earthly hour
She feels her love, the Spirit, in His power.

So late the Spring this year,
So high the angel mission sent to earth;
So wild the joy of her Elizabeth,
So strangely comforting her nephew's birth:
And now the coldest Winter ever known
Has left her here alone;
But for God whose Son she has just borne
And the Spirit filling her this happy morn.

Close as the star is distant,
   Its steady pulse beats with the heart of Heaven above;
Red as the rose is white,
   It beckons with the purity of new found love:

Yet even as she wraps him in a fleece,
She knows this is the dying of her peace.

DESERT SHIPS

The desert ships in file
Drawn by the comet's tail
As if it were a sail
Pad over waves of shale
As if God speeds them well.

What strangers bear
These cargoes rich and rare
Bought with craft and fear,
All death and fire,
In taverns drear?

A brooding king enquires
Of these strange seers,
Enforced ambassadors,
The fate of his desires
And half-known fears.

Oh! The relief of worship,
The fear of the return!

Unplighted troth
Unleashes murderous wrath:
Blood on the exile path:
Childless as Ruth,
They await a higher truth.

CHILDREN

A child escaped from Herod's sword
Did not escape the Roman tree;
Thus was the journey of Our Lord
From Bethlehem to Calvary.

And as we see him lying there
Or as he watches from the cross,
How far do we extend our care,
Repent the deed, make good the loss?

In every country children cry,
Abused and starved, tortured and killed:
No code for Christians to live by,
Not why He died, not what He willed.

Then for the Manger and the Cross
Strive to set every child free:
Love without a sense of loss
From Bethlehem to Calvary.

NATURE

The foxes brushed the dusty road
To smooth the path the donkey trod,
Bearing its light and precious load,
The mother and the son of God.

The shepherds, wakened by their sheep,
Heard angels' voices in the sky;
The cattle warmed the child in sleep,
Lowing a simple lullaby.

The camels signed a solemn truce
Of non-aggression with the kings
Who, solemnly, renounced abuse
And sighed for previous sufferings.

The ant, the lion and the dove
Gave thanks to Jesus in their way
But do I recognise his love
And offer mine to him each day?

PROPHESIES

Here is the most comfort that we can afford,
Rough flax for a peasant, not silk for a lord;
Let me lay you down quietly in the sweet hay
Which is not what the angel appeared to say.

Here are five fine shepherds enjoying their sport,
Music fit for a tavern but not for a court;
They have brought you a lamb from the flock's finest ewe
And yet it is tiny and weak just like you.

Here are seven grave sages who have followed a star,
Which has led them, they tell me, to just where we are:
They left their fine presents and fled in the night,
And we will be leaving as soon as it's light.

Here are eight fierce cavalry blocking our way,
At least they are Romans, not in Herod's pay;
And the more I reflect it seems Simeon was right,
And the angel seduced me with heavenly light.

Here are seventeen furlongs before the next bend,
The road of an exile seems never to end;
And if what Simeon told me is faithful and true,
What has happened to me will soon happen to you.

GOING BACK

Christmas Day 2012

Respectively intense or watered down,
Nostalgia flares to ignite worn desire,
As the outcast, lonely and depressed
Strain in the cold to boost the threadbare choir,
While the rational, who know that they know best,
Drink glühwein round an artificial fire.

The unfinished story of our Saviour's birth
Whispered by slaves in catacombs below
Imperial Rome, reached its imperial height,
Built on Victorian pomp and snow on snow,
Has morphed into its pagan origins,
Leaving a puzzling Christian after-glow.

And we, against the flow, move back in time
Towards the rebel church he came to found,
Of radical upheaval and reform,
Good news emerging from the underground,
Affirming not conforming, marginal
Because of what we say, both heterodox and sound.

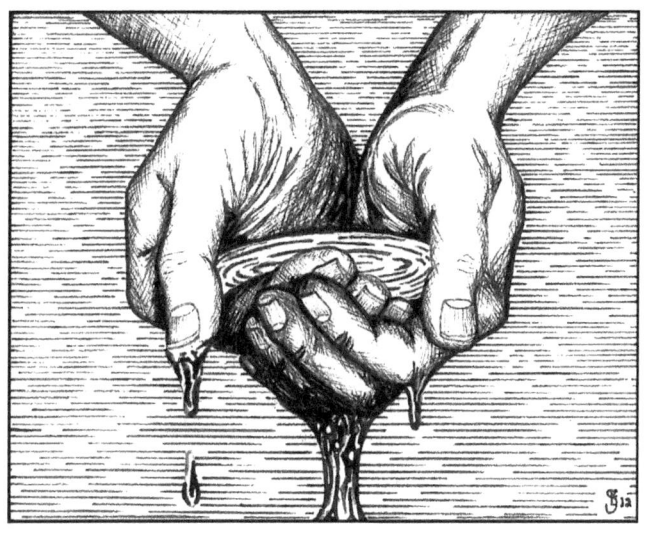

POST-EPIPHANY CAROLS

i. Dreams

When Joseph dreamed
He heard a sword shout
And felt the blood spurt
Over Ephrath;
And then he saw himself
A nomad
Beside a pyramid
Conning hieroglyphs.

Lulla, lulla, lulla-lulla.

When Caspar dreamed
He heard a prison
And felt a demon
In David's city;
Then saw three kings upon a byway
Far from the highway
Back to luxury.

Lulla, lulla, lulla-lulla.

When Herod dreamed
He felt a poison
And heard an orison
Deep in his palace;
Then saw himself eunuched in exile
Before a starry veil
Draped on a chalice.

Lulla, lulla, lulla-lulla.

When Jesus dreamed
He heard a choir
And felt the ardour
Of the Holy Spirit's Grace;
And then He saw the golden children,
Feted pilgrims
In His Father's warm embrace.

Lulla, lulla, lulla-lulla.
Lulla, lulla, lulla-lulla.

ii. Departure

Sadly set for Egypt, Mary says goodbye,
Knowing she must travel, scarcely knowing why;
Too tired and dusty to wipe a tear from her eye,
Doggedly determined, innocently shy.

Riding on a donkey through the barren wild,
Watchful and protective of her precious child;
Relieved but wondering what it will be like to be exiled
Infinitely patient, unfailingly mild.

No more homely shepherds, no more reverent kings,
Gone the wondrous stable and the birth star glittering;
And, taking each day as it comes, rooted or wandering,
Wedded to the mission of Gabriel's quickening.

iii. Massacre

Lost in the falling needles and the fading tinsel,
Buried in coloured paper and in turkey bones,
Not even shadows in our family rows and revels,
The Holy Innocents languish unmourned, unknown.

The earliest martyrs of our Church unconsecrated,
Killed between a pair of kings, too young to know,
The first Saints of the yet unwritten Second Covenant,
Of a line of victims reaping what they do not sow.

Now we have re-discovered Rubens graphic horror,
Remember the screaming sacrifice, the ruined mothers;
And in the name of He for whom they were slaughtered,
Suffer your children come to you; and all the others.

HONOUR ALL

Failing lights and dropping needles
Hardly fit to greet the kings,
Turkey soup and crusty Stilton,
Tired cards on sagging strings:
Christmas time that came too early
Ends in weary, bloated gloom,
Carols sung in late November
Fade as old routines resume.

Yet, as we watch with foreboding
As his presents are unpacked,
Jaded with our more than plenty
We should recall the things he lacked:
And as we resent the normal
We should walk his exiled way,
Grateful for the things we value,
Thankful for the quiet day.

May our purple, Advent season
Last until the holy night
When we sing our songs of greeting
Full of vigour and delight,
And may our extended season
Honour all that came to pass
From the Maid's Annunciation
To the Mother's Candlemas.

BRING YOUR CANDLES

Bring your candles for a blessing
Spreading light in home and heart;
Comfort in the nights of Winter,
With the glow that they impart:
Tranquil hours of contemplation,
Prayers to comfort, prayers to heal;
Giving warmth to friends and family
As we share a homely meal.

Light your candles happy Gentiles,
That same light which Simeon saw;
Warmth to melt the frost of duty,
Love to overwhelm the Law:
Light a candle for the mother
Whose light comforted Our Lord;
Light of holiness and beauty
In His Sacrament and Word.

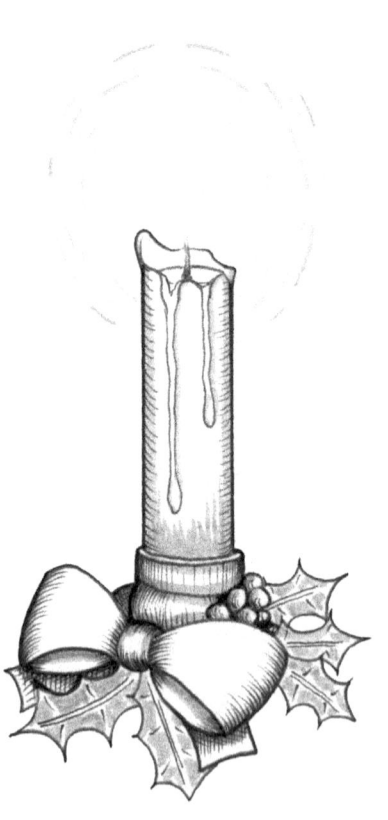

SIMEON'S DEATH

Out of the dark, the old man came,
Half hidden by the swirling smoke,
Then ghostly, etched in flaring flame,
He raised his claw-like hand and spoke.

In faltering phrases, near to death,
He said his dream had been fulfilled,
And, as if with his final breath
He said his hope had been fulfilled.

His hand reached out to take the boy;
She had no option but to yield;
And, far from filling her with joy
She dreaded what his words revealed.

The ritual carried out in haste,
Shocked and depressed, they hurried home,
A sword had pierced her gentle breast,
Thrust by Jerusalem or Rome?

She heard the old man died that night,
Exalted by her child's face;
She wished that she had seen the light
That lit him to his resting place.

SOLIDARITY

How did that petal brave the storm
To lie upon the snow like blood,
How did that eerie shadow form
A cross from random slats of wood?
How was it that the straw so sweet
Pricked sharp against a new child's skin?
How was it that the hostile street
Was proxy for the festive inn?

Why did the God of love who made
The world subject himself to earth?
And, if he must, a cavalcade
Should have announced his noble birth:
And why should ignominious death
Inflicted in return for grace
Have interposed between his breath
And his farewell to time and space?

Blood is the fuel which prompts the will,
Sluggish or fired as we are flawed,
By which we choose for good and ill
Craving the solace of our Lord;
And God, who made 'his' creatures good
That they might love 'him' true and free
Gave his sweet self in flesh and blood
In human solidarity.

THE APPLE WOOD OF CALVARY

The apple wood of Calvary
In sweet, sad smoke obscures the star,
Then upward drifts as frankincense
To meet the angels from afar:
Eve's virgin child awaits her child
While Joseph makes the manger good;
The tree, the carpenter, the Cross,
He chose to work in humble wood.

The bloody marble, rigid, cold,
Surveys the edict's cruel sneer
As Herod, flushed from banqueting,
Is surfeited with wine and fear:
The cry of innocents resounds
As Pilate mounts the judgment seat,
His hands within the marble bowl
Twist in the baptism of defeat.

But, then, the star above the cave
Marking the place where Jesus lay,
Obscured by clouds of heaven's rage
Upon that dark, redeeming day,
Serenely rose the following night
To see the tomb's disgorging grace,
The manger's promise ratified,
God's embassy in endless space.

PAGEANT

Distance from hardship leaves us uncomprehending
Less understanding than the truly poor;
Partly the distance between two points expanding,
Further and further from what went before
But partly through distancing from the real,
Preferring the abdication of the sentimental
To the degradation with which we ought to deal.
The poor still cry in broadcast tribulation
While we take refuge in religious art;
We know the skeleton of our divine salvation
But think it can survive without a heart.
What started as wild farce becomes a pageant
With gaudy shepherds facing splendid kings;
No room for ragged plebs and crooked agents
In the aesthetic way of showing things.
We stare through the eye of a needle at the scene
But do not know how hard it is to care;
Intent on understanding what has been
Instead of understanding what is here.
The way to narrow distance is to pray,
To leave room for the Spirit in our hearts,
To greet the unexpected every day
And learn acceptance as each day departs

IF I COULD WISH

If I could wish upon a star
It would not be for chocolate, or a racing car,
Or an electric guitar,
But for a peep
At Jesus fast asleep.

If I could travel near and far
It would not be to Xanadu or Shangri-la,
Or the Istanbul Bazaar,
But to stay
By the Christ child in the hay.

If I could hear the sweetest sound
It would not be *Beim Schlafengehen*, or the nightingale
Or *A Winter's Tale*,
But the baby's cry
Stilled by Mary's lullaby.

THEN AND NOW

The holy child so beautiful
Infused the darkness with a glow
That made the weary stable bright
But that was, oh, so long ago!

They say that angels filled the sky
Bringing good news to all mankind,
And then they sang a joyful song:
But we are oppressed and undermined.

His mother might have thought the gifts
Irreverent fruits of tyranny;
But nothing is too mean for them
To take from struggling folk like me.

And yet when Christmas Eve arrives
Our chronic troubles disappear:
The beauty glows in every heart
And lifts us for another year.

THEY BROUGHT JESUS!

They took us from our villages,
Our homes of creeper grass,
And stowed us, worse than animals,
A sick and dying mass;
They drove us into slavery
With the shackle and the lash,
No cruelty too terrible
To get their sugar cash:

But they were a miracle:
With their wickedness and greed
They brought Jesus.

They said that he was one of them
So they were 'specially blessed
But we knew he was one of us,
Black, harassed and oppressed:
The whites, like Romans, lived in style
His stable was a shack,
He died an innocent, like we died,
But, glory, he came back!

And he is a miracle:
From Calvary and the tomb
Arose Jesus!

GOOD CHEER!

Light the candles,
Dress the tree,
Put the crib upon the mantel.
Buy warm gifts,
Make provision,
Crown the baubles with an angel:

For Jesus is coming with light
On a Winter's night.

Merry face,
Arms embrace,
Love those whom you do not like.
Feed the lonely
At your table,
Break the tension with a joke:

For Jesus is the Word
Told to shepherds.

Enjoy gifts,
Raise a glass,
Everything for all who come:
Make some time,
Make some space,
Make your house into a home:

For Jesus is visited by kings
With exotic offerings.

Bring new hope,
Take new strength,
Plan to be a little better:
One more prayer,
One more smile,
One more offering for the stranger:

For Christ is with us all the year,
Good cheer.

THE ROSE

See the rose in Summer glory,
Bloom of the Creator's plan;
Symbol of the joy of Mary
When she carried God made man:
Hers the beauty grief could never
Tarnish as she faced the tomb,
Magnified in Christ forever
In the transformed upper room.

God whose love in incarnation
Broke the bonds of time and space
Through his Son for our salvation,
Comforter in our disgrace:
From his birth to crucifixion,
From the Cross to hell on earth,
Jesus suffers our infliction,
Source and witness of new birth.

Spirit of Christ's consummation,
Source of life when all seemed lost,
In the words of consecration
And the fire of Pentecost:
Help us honour all creation,
Live the Kingdom hour by hour;
Filled with hope and expectation
Of the Triune love and power.

MISTELTOE AND HOLLY

My berries soft and white
Of timeless love
Embracing an old oak
In floating mist:
Kissing and kissed.

My berries bright and red
Of timeless love
Embracing all mankind
In pain and death
The Spirit's breath.

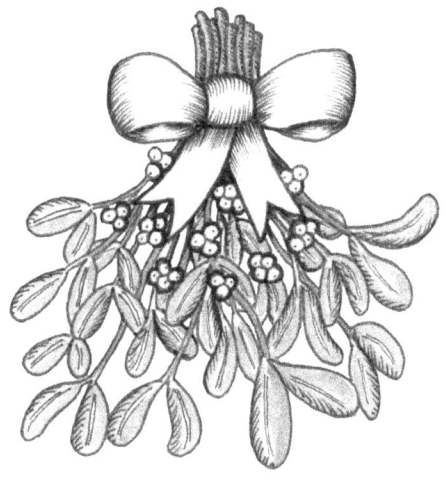

But where I am so gentle
You bear a prickle.

Your vaunted timeless love
Will not sustain
Without pain.

I gave my blood in love
For evermore,
For the unlovely and the poor:
Faces not dressed in mist
Shall still be kissed.

PETALS

A white petal lying in the straw,
A mother and her infant O so pure;
A tableau so quiet and so poor,
And yet it changed the world forevermore.

A pink petal floating on the lake,
Of fish and of souls a mighty take;
They could not believe it on the shore:
And yet it changed the world forevermore.

A red petal nailed upon a tree
The most precious blood in history
Poured out, negating what had gone before:
And so it changed the world forevermore.

A golden petal floating in the wind
Between the earth and sky for all mankind,
A mystery to worship and explore:
Because it changed the world forevermore.

VIRGIN OF THE RAJ

Virgin of the Raj
Geisha full of Grace
Bearer of Our Lord
For all God's human race:
Mother of the sick
Sister of the poor
Sheds a lonely tear
Outside the stable door.

Exile in the dust
Wanderer in the heat
Home at Calvary
To see His last defeat:
Servant of the dead,
Waitress at the board
In the upper room
Heard of the risen Lord.

ON BEAUTY

i.

Where beauty subtly warms the aching heart,
Seeming more pliant, mere prettiness hurts;
Thus, snow which hides the blemishes of earth
Wraps cruel fingers round a doubtful birth.

And, come the ugly thaw, bedraggled mess
Asserts itself, though something is amiss;
A shard of beauty lights the drizzling day
Transmitted from the manger where he lay.

iii.

The smooth, heroic elegance of rhyme
Unchecked by assonance betrays the theme;
Beauty is in the jaggedness of things,
Not in the smooth abstractedness of dreams.

The danger of Demosthenes is to speak
Where substance is subjected to technique;
Beauty is found less in the poetry
Than in Luke's story of Nativity.

ii.

Dull and worn out, sky, clothes and wood,
Insipid shabbiness from swaddling to shroud;
But then, Renaissance paint depicting light
Excludes the dull and champions the bright.

The grey of lowering skies and smoking lamp,
Fabric uncertain in its dye; and limp
Give way to shepherds bright in pink and green,
And Mary, blue as sapphire, Fairy Queen.

While hidden light heroic birth
The essence of its heroism is dearth;
In art technical facility must protect
Beauty from the snare of mere effect.

CHRISTMAS TOWN

Jesus calls the reindeer in,
Wise men huddle on a sleigh,
Joseph drinking at the inn,
Robins nesting in the hay:
Snow men line the empty street
Where the star is shining down,
Santa and the shepherds meet,
In the square of Christmas town.

Herod at his market stall
Selling gold and silver crowns,
"Jingle Bells", the angels call,
Filling sacks in dressing gowns,
Chestnuts roasting on the fire
In the stable snug and warm,
Joseph practising the lyre,
Jesus in his mother's arms.

Santa brings a load of straw,
Jesus Christ pretends to sleep,
Presents on the stable floor,
Will he dare to take a peep?
All the elves begin to sing,
Santa reverently kneels down,
Everyone is worshipping
Christ the King of Christmas Town.

MARY'S CHILD

i. EVE

When Eve turned her face for the last time
To look back at the 'tree of sin',
God thought she had never looked so beautiful,
Even though skins defaced her naked skin.

"Love out of adversity and loss
Is better than the heavenly bland:
They will love me and each other heroically,
Not mindlessly obeying my command.

"A father cannot help naive love;
But I knew that it could not last:
The garden was always too good to be true
Lacking a bright future from a dark past.

ii. THE SPIRIT'S FIRE

The spring and poise of young flesh
Tenses in sudden radiance,
Fixed like a marble sculpture,
Arrested in a girl's dance.

Her ears swelling with heartbeat,
She hears the voice within her;
How can Zion's Messiah
Be carried by a sinner?

The voice gently caresses
And fills her with desire;
She opens all her senses
And feels the Spirit's fire.

iii. PRESENTS

A walk into the barren hills
Away from harsh tongues whispering;
News of two cousins soon to come;
The herald and the people's king.

A Nazarite and Nazarene,
Remembering how the message came,
—She puts her hands below her breasts—
The outward light, the inward flame.

Her cousin, glowing with new life,
Repeats the words the angel said;
Then Mary sings old Hannah's song,
The poor raised up, the hungry fed.

Bound in God's hope they know their joy
Beyond the confines of their day,
Their bodies' presents to the world,
Their place in sacred history.

iv. BABY CLOTHES

Fine silk for a saviour,
The fabric of kings,
Bright and soft as butter
As it falls and clings.

Yes, linen is better!
It fits nice and tight
Around a new master
On a Winter's night.

Wool is well enough,
So soft and springy
The very stuff
For a new baby.

Then cotton bindings
Will have to do;
Like funeral windings:
And good day to you!

v. COLD

Snow like a lacen mantle drapes itself
Upon the shoulders of the ancient town;
Lending a transient beauty to the squalid,
    Whitening black as it comes down.

But they who feel its bite know the illusion,
    The doubtful elegance for a celebration;
The stable door wedged tight against the chill,
    Against the cruel beauty of creation.

The swaddled infant laid within the manger,
    His mother huddles in her temperate stuff;
They have no money to provide for Winter
When all their clothing would not be enough.

A cruel gust knifes through the flimsy slats;
The baby, cold and frightened, starts to cry;
His mother gives him all the warmth she has,
    A breast, a kiss, her cloak, a lullaby.

vi. GIFTS

You might say all gold is the same,
Calibrated by volume and quality;
But I know its nerves, blood and veins,
Its mood swings and subtlety:
Not that bar; there was blood in the mine.
The monarch that I have in mind
Would only want to see it shine
And never trade nor melt nor grind.

Frankincense is more subtle still
As it varies according to tree,
At what height and what slope of the hill:
The priest designated to burn
This offering is one of a kind,
And so we must carefully discern
A fragrance for his cast of mind.

Myrrh is often dismissed as a waste
But no corpse will be rarer than this
Metamorphosing earthly distaste
Into untrammelled heavenly bliss:
For whom? We are sure of the birth
Of a child - all our tables agree -
Who will come down from heaven to earth
And set all of humanity free.

vii. WIZARDS

Like a magnet in the sky	Like a savage lunatic,
The star conducts a desperate race:	Herod simpers, snarls and slides:
Climb to pine	"Find the child,
Plunge to palm,	Bring me word.
Nestling farm,	Double dealing?
Barren space.	How absurd!"

Like a fever on the ground	Like a weight endured for years
The people shout and grasp and curse:	Cargo slaps the dusty stone:
Camels haunched,	Gold and Myrrh
Money thrown,	And Frankincense,
Mistrust sewn	Star intense,
Hard to reverse.	Then disappears.

Like a life complete at last,
Wizards' final spells are cast:
Worshipping
The infant king
Future blossom
Rooted past.

viii. WHERE?

Where is the sword to pierce my heart?
I only hear my baby cry
And what he needs I can supply:
Where is the sword?

Where is the grief that summons tears?
The old man smiles his prophesy
Touching my boy, looking at me:
Where is the suffering?

I know it, like the dead of night.
All that I pray for is a stay,
No hope of sorrow going away;
We only lack the year and day.
I know.

ix. MARY'S ENGLAND

Mary's infant carried high
Over the shingle band
To mellow England;
Through the mist
Jesus Christ
Borne on his muddy way
Through mossy England.

Safe from Herod's murderous bands,
Safe from scarred and cruel hands,
In the dappled, grassy lands
Of melancholy England.

Ah! But woe was the day
Through the thunder and spray
When they went on their way
From lovely England:
For they raised him on high
On a cross there to die
But his last, saving cry
Reached Mary's England.

EU GPSR Authorized Representative:

LOGOS EUROPE, 9 rue Nicolas Poussin, 17000 La Rochelle, France

contact@logoseurope.eu

www.ingramcontent.com/pod-product-compliance
Lightning Source LLC
Chambersburg PA
CBHW070451050426
42451CB00015B/3434